what you used to wear

CHARMAINE CADEAU

what you used to wear

Edited by Anne Simpson.
Cover photograph: *Wood Island, Grand Manan,* 1998,
copyright © Alison Hughes, heidih@nb.sympatico.ca
Cover and interior design by Julie Scriver.
Printed in Canada by AGMV Marquis.
10 9 8 7 6 5 4 3 2 1

National Library of Canada Cataloguing in Publication

Cadeau, Charmaine, 1977-
What you used to wear / Charmaine Cadeau.
Poems.
ISBN 0-86492-410-0

I. Title.

PS8605.A34W43 2004 C811'.6 C2004-903171-6

Published with the financial support of the Canada Council for the Arts, the Government of Canada through the Book Publishing Industry Development Program, and the New Brunswick Culture and Sports Secretariat.

Goose Lane Editions
469 King Street
Fredericton, New Brunswick
CANADA E3B 1E5
www.gooselane.com

For my family

contents

what you used to wear

Ladders

Take this girl on one-lane roads
and across the lighted bridge.

Take her past the old sugar bush
where leaves drop into open-mouthed pails,

camouflaged in rust. If you can, abandon
gardens where wagon wheels

are propped against houses, or rain barrels
spill chrysanthemums. The lawns are lined

with embarrassed cars exposing their parts
in long grass. In one yard, a vintage

gas pump, a wire coop. Leave behind churches,
now family-of-four homes glowing with fluorescent

lights and satellite TVs. Take her to any number
of groves scattered across this country

where someone has hammered
planks onto trunks, rising to branches

in uneven steps. Think of the builder
who knows these corners, who tends

to the treetops, mythic and green.
The view is good from here.

The potter

For the mud floor to be sacred ground,
call for a ploughshare retired from the furrow
or signs of where the chaff was held.

The timber frame rasps at night and wears
its age in gaps, but the threshing
barn had space for the slip

and wheel, rows of draft-dried pots,
the largest one a flayed kettledrum.
The potter meadows his fields,

dandelions and crabgrass,
works the earth in handfuls
spinning slabs of clay in tilted rounds

keeping flat the bases. Above him, knots
are portholes to navigate by the stars,
funnelling what the sky can't hold

so as not to lay waste. But what it is that
welters in rainwater, lagging in the belly
of one – a feather fallen from the rafters,

petals blown in from the apple trees, a spider
drowned, a reflection of yourself,
if nothing else.

Gathering tobacco

Or was it the train that darkly stumbles
past the drying barn on uneven

tracks? Mortared logs are tight fingers
the colour of soot and dusk.

The tobacco pickers who pinch
the ripe green left the leaves to fade

inside the walls, tumbling together
in sighs like soft collisions of moths

netted with the kitchen glow. Not even they,
climbing the glass in verticals,

glide in the rattle of the thickly cased night.
Saliva will mute the June bugs

that throw the windows awake.
Roll them moist with tongue and teeth

but first preserve their wings
between some pages

because they move like eyelids
during sleep; translucent blinks

that will set loose a spark if
clicked fast enough. Or wait

for the silence that morning offers
when they quietly hang like weights,

magnetic against the soft-haired,
pale underside of leaves.

Open air

Tightly bound like a sultan's hair, heavy with musk,
hay turns aphid green in drought light.

The shafts cut down, crops become secondary
to the violet appetite of flowers. Ripe clover,

soft as skin, is fit for a bed in the loft.
Earthswept, the bales are spaced apart like workers

spread out in the heat of the day with no retreat
of shade and still as the sun burns each, patches

of dark come like mirages, untouchable
shadows. Spun like snail shells kept

in a mason jar, curved like the ear pressed
against the farmer's chest at night,

he imagines the bales undone, lying flat
on the ground, tight-fitted with the earth again.

Nearby, the wind moves the wild
rye along the roadside. A gust of seeds

catch in stiff bulrushes assembled in the culvert.
Milkweed empties white down

floating to rewrite Newton's laws
and the grey paper shells left on the stem

hang like wasp nests,
flagging consequence and harvest.

Coronet

On Constantine's crown
an unknown woman
dances among four
birds, one tilting
above her shoulder.
Dark vines enclose them,
and she makes room to move.

She holds a scarf,
serpentine and savage,
above her head
clutching the ends
in her hands. Her slippers
are worn nearly bare in circles
where her feet touch ground.

The smell of rosewater
lingers in her hair
as she turns without romance or
artifice, one foot raised,
all joy weighted
in the other,
ready to leap.

Safe as houses

The patron of desperate cases
rests in her chair, embroiders a camisole,
and thinks of the next blessing
of roses. She knows how we are all assured

of miracles. Along the highway, pasture rose,
and close to her a horse runs in its field
keeping pace with a car. A loose-hinged gate
swings open and the grass bends along the ankles

of the fence. Woven flower of braided hair, a garden
of tripwires of delicate thread tying leaf to
leaf, the spider crouching, dusted in pollen.
The uncovered well at the back of the lot is

floored with thousands of copper
pennies. Dark tea settles into hairline cracks
that thin into midnight in a bone china cup;
the cup, showing a picture of lupines on its side.

Laundry

The clothes froze
on the line overnight
showing the musculature
of the wind,
how they shifted
in the laps of the gods, erect.
Wild frost drew branches
heavy with snow on the glass,
a fine muslin
the sun drank blue.

Long division

Everything reduced
to weathervanes and birdhouses,
the rail that stretches longer today
from this house to the next,
as if any of these things
can tell you about the people
here. The rusted love of an old wire
holding the fence together
smudges pale wood at the nails,
separates you from the watching
trees and field where wild turkeys
hunch in a line of silhouettes
preparing for the evening's stretch
from ground to branch.

Circulation

I'm not afraid of you not wanting me,
only of what we call circumstances.

Mornings like this, I'd rather have rain
and stay flannelled in bed, invite

the silent umber beasts that stave
the walls to keep us company.

Bridged, atrial, we turn from the clock
as starlings spill from the line, awakening.

We talk of yesterday, sweeping
twigs and nests from the eaves,

how you cupped thin blue
eggs, fearless, in your palms.

Breast stroke

On the mountain
clouds rush by
in flexes of muscle
rubbing shoulder to shoulder.

The quiet herd
grazes our bodies,
hooves the lake's surface
so we strip down

to swim beneath them.
Each long stroke
raises us up,
purgatorial, between wind

and water and clouds.
The burnt offerings
of our flesh pricking beneath
small jewelled lakes

splinter the shoreline.
The light descends
and white lowers its head
into a half-blush.

Winter

Along tight vistas, streets of painted houses,
he tips into the wind and snow, a portrait

of fidelity. His black umbrella shades him
from the searching gods, ignorant of this disguise.

A dilated pupil, a syncopated note on a staff,
the terrestrial pole around which others move down

the sidewalks, scarved chests, coattails drawn out.
Pelting their faces, snowflakes melt on contact.

The flies this season

Camphor and locks: and this is home
to a sunworn few. Hounds that clamour
in the dark to raccoon song
drown out the buzz and twitch of tired flies
that always come this time of year. Invited
in through holes and cracks of walls
insulated with newspapers and horsehair, loose
windowpanes, or the front door swinging
again unlatched, they storm against the hot
glass of light bulbs, finding their way beneath
shades and fixtures. The older ones ricochet
from walls like slow-motion BBs
until they die, at last humming out
freedom. Lying on their backs, red-goggled
eyes turn down towards the sill
or counter or floor. Legs and dendrite wings
are released to stir in the drafts of our
movements, catch on the sleeve of a sweater.

Migration

A flock of geese
pull a corner of sky south
between their dark bodies,
bending wings
that drum softly on their sides.
They are folding it
beyond the cedars
like a sheet
fresh from the line.
Snowshoe tracks leading here
are wide-billed,
curved like rabbit snares;
the ends are memory
pointing home.
Leaves trapped in ice
sojourn until spring,
while dogwood & sumac
hold red in their throats,
cinders glowing.
I fear losing
myself inside this second home
as a heart grown thin
may slip through ribs.

The drying room

How we are taken and kept
I half understand
in the fugitive light.

The preserve jars below the herbs,
tied and hung in bundles from bent nails,
were here since the hum of cicadas

swelled and withdrew wave after wave
and there was nothing to do (my fingers
wet in the basin after washing

the blackberries) but cut back the basil
and bay leaves. The taste and smell
of that afternoon knocks like the shutters

against the house, urges like an insect
bristling in the cage of my hands,
long-winged and impatient.

This is my body

The caned grasses
shake in the ditch
like dry bones
in a medicine bag;
a jarful of frogs
left in the rushes –
muscle. The hesitant light
peering through branches
throws a web
of nerves across them.

At the reserve

Wetness sluices our paddles
as we lift them from the bog,
transport in its pulse.

Beneath us, lush red tendrils caress
the hull of the canoe, issuing
hush as we drift. Dimpling the surface,

darting in straight lines – water spiders –
like our boat, draw maps in brief ribbons.
The dragonfly hovers over tamarack and

sunken trees. Markings on a turtle,
tightly shelled, mirror the yellow lilies
that, needing light and water, graze

the edges of both. Isolation
only lasts until carp begin to spawn
ahead of us, a furious silver knot

of fins and scales. As each undulation
heaves, we're left wanting to entangle
ourselves in anything, in each other.

Painting trees, totems

You swapped secrets with Ucluelet, sinking
a piece of the shore's grey
welcome in your pocket to grow warm against
your leg, a salve drawing out venom, parted
lips circling your skin. The arbour haze,
like pictures of sunken ships,
barnacled, heavy, lost,
was home. And in the green
among trees slim like matchsticks, you felt
small, shoes dipping into the wet ground.
You held your breath to see
if here, beneath their weight, you'd
stop and thump out a final beat.
But a tree, curving and full,
drew you in with the sun
tasting auburn and ginger –
trapped light in glimpses –
the quick snap, then bloodless, broken.

Green Comma

Banish me to where the birches
surrender their leaves to hunger,
and the canopy is thick with holes
like the old covered bridge in Montrose.
The patches of sky mend it a thousand
times with sunset, stars. White softwood falls
from a whittling branch shaved in imperfect
circles, Queen Anne's Lace and ferns.
The knife gives shape not to butterflies,
but to twilight. A small totem
of bear and wolf, turtle and hawk.
Dimness strikes a face, says
I've suffered, I.

Signs other than miracles

In suffering, the crux
of the thing: half-opened eyes,
the curve of a broken body,

swung neck. One felt
what it was to have humble beginnings,
filth and poverty

next of kin. The anguish they fell for,
or blood from the rack,
gave them a taste,

dispensing final breaths,
the heavy ache of insult
in the back of the throat, a need

to see moments of death.
Each atrophied from playing
at acts of God once,

they felt small, waiting.
Ironic, maybe, when
your hands are pinned in place.

Luck in the mines

The ground is hungry yet.
I fed the garden bulbs in spring
but it delivered them back
green. These hollow shoots
bend away from us, arching
in curves like ribs,
shying away from hands
trowelling its gardens.

Left to the yard, we watch as insects
hollow cavities beneath us
giving their hearts more room to echo
and thump. We study civilizations of ants,
a mud wasp that emerges from the ground
guarding the entrance to below
where eggs shine like eyes in the dark.

Wharf

The water nudges a moored rowboat,
tired fins shadow the bottom of a pail,

a hand cuts a length of rope at the knot,
and the unsettled bones of the weir stretch

up into sight. A man in waders and a uniform
scrubs the spray-painted confessions

of nighttime lovers from the rocks
with a bucket and a laundry brush

while anonymous bathers watch as the waves
dissolve blue and red. Crooked

hearts are the hardest to wash away,
next to percent signs

and fletching. He knows love
as it has been written here, as it has

been carved in picnic tables, or scratched
in the obvious skin of rest-station trees.

Tokens

You kept the glass pebble
from the beach for years.
When you held it up
to weigh the colour
you imagined a bottle,
hermetic and slim,
how it was passed around the table
and emptied between friends.

Sucking the cool deep into delicate lung
and, tiring in the waves,
touching down against the hard slate, flat
shield. Undressing first, the label lifted off intact.
Split against the rocks, the water
was salve for these injuries, licking
until smooth and setting this piece ashore.

Waves in the cylinder glass of the window
that you trimmed with lace
screened the view of the birch.
Overlooking the yard,
jars stood on the sill, one hand-blown,
blue green blue
at different heights.
All held the half-light of the morning.

Because the pebble blurred
like the green speed from a train,
you remembered the smell of home
and how death, how absence changed it.

Natural selection

We move from room to room
like garage sale lampshades,

vaguely dim, somewhat gaudy.
The taste of four-letter words
in our throats is confessional:

candour has mortared these walls.
Stiff palms from church

that were sprinkled
with holy water
are tucked behind pictures

marking years of Sundays
and the times we thought to

bless this house.
We had to keep them
uncertain of the sin of disposal.

Flight

The city is green steepled and calm,
words strung like beads worn close
to the skin to count and recount and
the nearest we get to heaven today
is in seeing a distant osprey
lift its wings, prepare for passage,
bear all the weight of our imagining.

Traffic

The dusted print of collision
hung in translucent wing and tail
on the bedroom window. Outdoors,
nothing on the ground. Birdsong shook
from the timberline, its path
a white scar of exposed roots.

Morning at the market

A boat drifts frictionless,
a paper lantern dimly lit.
Pallets of fish
limp, marble-eyed,
leak onto pavement.
One man, hanger thin,
each limb wire drawn, precise,
sells dried fruits
shrivelled like doused stars.
He wraps a carp in newspaper,
tucking the tail under neat corners.
I hold its weight under my arm,
carrying the ashamed body
like a handbag.

Gallery after midnight

On the top floor
of a rough stone building
a bat flutters
around the works
of Thomson and Varley
setting off an alarm,
bringing the police.
We are glad for
moments of intrusion
and sleeplessness,
relieved to find the universe
so loosely bound.

Silos, dirt roads

We drive east, wheels
kicking up dust, Cimarron spirited,

beside cornfields and wheat fields,
a patronage of crows. Publicity.
The flapping leaves wave us on

as we pass. We're unwelcome here, politely
rushed through, so stopping in this ordered

cosmos – everything equally
spaced apart – has a certain appeal. There's no
obvious point of entry. The wall of corn

resists passage but we push through, bending
the stalks, braceleted in green. This is a reunion.

Tracing

In summer, grey rocks
along the riverbank
are too hot to touch.
Yet one by one
quiet snakes
stretch out in increments
comparing themselves
length to length.
One casts off its skin
when it slips through cracks
leaving it whole
and intact, like a wind serpent
resting from flight, for a moment
visible. The transparent body
is torn at the corners
of the mouth – a slight
splitting that all departures
are bound to have.

Sand dunes

What sleeps among hills of bone
and grit leaves impressions of its scales
feathered and winding in the dunes
that curve to fit this shored
body. The wind will erase the halcyon
myth, smoothing the lines as if to make the bed
fresh again. You sift grains
between your fingers
and study the phrenology of these hills,
divining impulse, sense, or tenderness.
A slender-billed curlew bends its neck
as you sink to the ground's history
regressus ad uterum.
Preparing for sleep,
the heavy-headed oat grass
nods towards the earth.

Fixed in limestone

Fossil. Light wears down
chill bone. You want to toss a shawl
over exposed grief. She flinches
before the tail is patient again.
She has no rights. The body
only tallies loss. She tries to remember
sky as it looked under bowing lake,
a keel's waterlines, lacewing sinking.

Lakescape

Shiver and ask
whether the lake soaked through each
of her barkless rings,
only half-buried. Line in the sand, she rifts
the beach in a trip of roots
and trunk, snagging your eye
in a landing-net sweep.
When at last she claws her way out
from below the lake, her arm
stretches nine feet in the air,
grabs seagulls from the sky
and chokes the pitch of their calls.
Between the crook of her
elbow and shore
lap mussels, halved,
clacking like mandibles.
When tongues loosed,
shells shocked white
as though they witnessed
their souls leave them.
If they had seemed more than milk teeth,
Canopic jars that hold sand,
or pieces of chalk
to scribble down words
otherwise hard to wash away,
you may have let them rest.

But as it is you pick them up,
wanting to layer them like scales
over bare skin.
Needing to see what it is
to wear your bones
on the outside.

Lunar white

If anything, be granted a blunt ending.
Given time enough, your fingers
pressed to your neck
would count the beats
and forecast the last
almost apologetically,
as though this is just another time
you didn't deliver what we had hoped,
our disappointed faces shining like moonstone.

We gambled on fine weather.

Your heart, your fist,
relaxed when the apple trees were in full bloom
in the Annapolis Valley.
Wisdom twists long in their strange trunks
favouring character over beauty.
You climbed the ladder to get a better look.
The farm was yours
when you spent nights by lamplight
tying small feathers to hooks,
inventing insects to fasten to your vest,
careful not to snag your fingers.
Always too large, too rough.

You asked your nurse
for the mare, wanting the dark muzzle
to nudge you for a brand of love
free from resentment.
You obliged as you did when she chose to veer,
gave up the whip and reins.

We sent saddle oil instead of flowers
to your bedside
knowing you would prefer the smell.

Five horses drowned one year
in the river you learned to fish,
learned the trick of keepnets.
Funny that a surgeon would set one in your chest,
it held together for more than twenty years.
In her mane, your hands read knotwork
that spelled the stirring of waves.
Leaving us for some world of grace,
you at last undid the heart's knot.

Becoming

The blistering feathers on a red-winged
blackbird shows where the sun, wanting flight,
was lured in and held snug against pale skin.
The hunter's wife watches the cedar rail
as the wing looks to bleed,
loose down on the cracked earth.

In a moment, bird is smudged in shadow,
preening on the fence, sucking
each feather clean in his mouth,
turning wings into fans to find the body cool.

Half-nude in the kitchen,
the grease in the air from the griddle
slides into her skin like perfumed oil.
Maybe then rain.

The fourth of my anxieties

The maze was wet and there you stood
mistaking leaf for feather, thinking flight,
and seconds took you far,

and me, defenceless. Apart, how quickly
one forgets the drop
of forgiving shoulders, and finds comfort

instead in rituals of sleep;
warms milk in a black-bottomed pot,
folds mint leaves in a white linen square,

and, placing it beside a pillow, dreams
of trading the smell of street vendor stalls
and sawdust to walk downwind of you.

After dancing

The night was gowned, perfumed,
the moon white like a hand slipping
tortoise-shell combs in at the nape
to hold her hair in place.

On her wrist, petals, their dark folds bruising.
A testament. The humid night
rubbed across their faces.

By the front porch, she said,
"Something has been eating the roses."

You had seen enough
by the time she closed the door,
the perforated leaves.

Where we step softly

The sun made tall shadows of us
and the trees
bending towards the moraine,
vertebral. Birch skin lifts like wallpaper
revealing former selves,
their nude interiors tempting
us to peel the bark
further. Tongues of lichens
soothe the cool rocks
bedded in brushwood and moss.
In the stirring
branches, nuthatches are piping
small notes of relief.

A certain direction

The muted script of tracks in snow
is set off by a red fox who carries
the weather on the tip of his tail,
as though he's newly painted this scene
white and is filling in the vacant spaces
left by hooves and claws. He noses
the ground for small-boned life, deciphering
a smattering of brown feathers dropped
from the sky that stick up like quill pens in
ink wells. Imagine how it would look to see
the maps of our lives flattened like this
as an unsteady hand charts the sprints
and pauses, leaving room for mistakes.

An umbrella blew inside out in October

We began with today's law of gravity,
that the curve of this planet and the combined
weight of our bodies allowed us to be
tossed together. Factor in the wet streets,
how we were guided by the ugly nudity of
lawn-choked earthworms and loose-ribbed rainwater
thrumming sewer grates. Among the sonatinas
of drops pelting aluminum trash cans,
we learned something of the geography
of towns built on hills, with what ease
things are willing to descend, be tugged through
seasons unquestioning. The strain of returning
home uphill wasn't half as bad if we allowed for
our susceptibilities, the stubborn, dead leaves
that would cling to branches all winter long.

Toeing the water from makeshift docks

The small islands are the thumbholes
of this place, the ones left off maps
without even local names to recommend them.
Unexplored piles of primeval rock and tree
are eased without bird to interfere,

without someone barefoot
resting beneath the wind-warped branches.
Crowded evergreens that lean over water
plan for gradual escape.
Or are they slanting as we do

when watching someone leave,
cocking our heads and bowing forward
as if these small adjustments
could let us follow beyond doorways,
along a crowded street?

A tree on the shore releases its roots from granite
and tipping in, steers the lake, heavy and full,
will drift until its voyage is marked
in tangles of algae, etched with wormholes
that curl progress in shallow, bending loops.

Thunderstorm

Since the rain began
we've waited and watched
the rough sex of the lake
bucking the boats
against the dock. Across the water,

a bright finger of lightning
strokes a tree.

A hundred years of life burns
for days.

We follow the smoke
wanting to see how patience
thins to black.

These shores

A water beetle stutters out
the last of his complaints
along the patio stones. He shines,
like the lake, paddled and gilled,
black bodied in the dark.
A seam of shell splits open to wings,
dizzying beats. Moonlight reflects from
the white scales of a fish
rising to the surface. Closing
struggle of a damp piece of night
twisting legs, hinges, breath.

The way back

Water pours down the cliffs
to the lake where we stand waist-deep
in water running our fingers in the grooves

of petroglyphs. We decipher the shapes.
This, an antler, this, a procession.

The nests of swallows above us
invent caves on the rock face,
shelve the coast in beds.

You are not so domestic.

Rendering the universe

The sea rests on the back
of the wind, channelling between shoulder
blades and settling in the curve of the lower

spine. The river presented
options: drink, wash, float. It carried
your sea urchin heart helpless in the current.

You, resting in a tub, white steam,
white porcelain fogging the window,
water on your body in rain shapes.

Catching hold

You awoke with your chin
tucked to your chest
like a locket, or the sorts
of flowers that lower
themselves at night, folding in.
Pressing your mouth against
her morning lips,
you eat every syllable,
the long vowels
sinking to your stomach like rocks.

West wind

You welcome necessary rescues
when you are filled with granite thirst,
when you were shy on the mountain.
The wind took hold of you
in its giant palm,
lifted you down the crags,
your body grazing the ground.
You could have been dropped,
falling headfirst, not trusting
yourself to flight
but you touched down in a field
of wildflowers that breezed
against the length of you. You slept
with your face pressed in cornbells
and woke up in a house
you'd never seen before, married
to a man who would come to you
only in the dark. Even so, you were
better off than your sisters
so the rest of the story doesn't matter.

Vaseline glass and whale oil

In the sedge light of the lamp,
you were hinterland and cove,

telling stories of how you once trapped
animals and tamed them to keep

in the yard. A rabbit would trust
itself to your hand, smoothing

back its ears, eyes
closing, pulse breathing into yours.

You learned familiarity as a breed
of dependence, saw love moving

without language or skepticism.
A pair of swans nested in the shed

one winter. Remembrance closed
around them, a doorknocker,

cold and fixed. We imagined
the story ending with the worst

death. You said it is terrible to look
at private moments.

Circumstances

The remains
of the bridge
rise like stilts
from the river,
bases marked
for the boats.
Tracks lifted
from struts
one by one,
uncollectible,
the passage,
an abyss.
A balance is
found under
the absence
of the train.
Water rusts
trestles into
quiet copper.

Sundays

There is integrity in the whitewashed planks
and bowing roof of this country church,
slumping in the mud of cornfields.
Someone's hands must patch
the leaks, light the furnace, and paint the
walls fresh each spring. Erupting
like teeth, gravestones push
up through the palate of the earth. Blanched
prayers hunch among the glacier cut hills, where
a shiver of purple strife waits.

Reincarnation

I imagine how it would be
to come into this world,

this body,
a second time.

To be born in captivity
or wake up naked,

fetal in the lobe of an oyster shell
sputtering out sand.

To be released
from the soft grey skin of

a milkweed pod
and land with both feet

on the ground
or for death and birth

to converge in the
bright bloom of a star.

Shifting ice

A small feeling took shelter
in the feathering ear of the owl

waiting on the post. We stayed
inside as much as possible

that winter against the fields
shocked into rest with white,

armoured ourselves
in something like the translucent

shells of crayfish left on the shores
in July, tiny joints repeating

down the tails. The tectonic
movement of ice on the river

creaked no more than the branches
along the banks, pieces swept

into piles by the current. A river of
sharp beaks, gaping eyes.

Clearing the lot

Outside, autumn smoke
heaves a year of brush and
vines, wet leaves
stuffed into an old oil drum
growing fat in the field.
Ash rises from self-conscious
flame. The slightest
breeze would rip this taffeta, pieces
darting like so many crickets
prophesying what's to come.

Fallen things

No straight lines to lead you
through the back country
thick with mosquitoes,
bundles of twine and wire. A mare
drops her head to the green plate
by the fence of blasted roots,
a line of antlers. Dinner time,
and look how they gather.

Acorns

The neighbour's children
are writing shallow letters
in the earth, fingering its dryness
with long grey sticks
found in the undergrowth.
The benevolent ground,
a long-ignored pet
being scratched behind its ears,
spoken to in soothing tic tac toes.
Should a deer on its way to the white
cedar lot cross the yard,
the sticks will drop in the dirt.
Language will begin again.

Filling pockets

Take what you can.
There is no enemy here
(stones that brighten
when wet, a beached jellyfish
that flattens near your feet,
afterbirth) except for a brow,
the shoal that says
not down, not down yet.
The late summer ocean
presses itself into
the sand beneath it,
leaves traces of nerves
in shadows and curving lines,
and above, transparent
bells move with a sense
of frailty. Pocket some
shells, a feather,
the kelp, the claws.
This is your continent.

What I'd say

That we could go to the scrapyard when it rains
and claim it as our own percussive concert,
strut barefoot in mudflats, wear flies
like proud jewels on our earlobes
and throats, give proper names to all
numbered streets, or, lie in a field
where the grass is supple enough
to retain the imprints of our bodies
long after we leave.

Bush supposed a bear

Walking by the blue spruce
and the best you can do
is finger the plastic whistle
you tied to a string

while you remember
the broad, dark figure
at the natural history museum.
You know something of signposts,

even admire how the roughworn trees
are chewed and scratched
like well-loved bedposts, like overblown
tinder whittled for a fire,

or used-up restaurant toothpicks
spit out on the sidewalk.
The bark bristles like scales
lifting onto the blade of a fishing

knife, feathers pricking up for a mating
dance. A black bear tried to dig
four dens this fall but every time hit
solid rock. Call for the wind

to yank out this tree, make him a home
where rocks mimic his posture
and slope into the hills. Fish are born
for him, shaped by the white foam

of the stream. The ground will sacrifice
sedge and clover to his winter appetite.
He'll rest in this place, tucked in a dark seam
on a bed of hemlock beneath the stars,

escaping your cartography,
the contours of a heart, the arc
of an explorer's footprint,
systems of enclosure.

Mill town

We, too, are rolled in dust, and try to scrub
our fingernails clean. Near the quarry, cedar
roots drag the ground, lift scattered bones

of pioneers. Bees are drawn to the purple buds
of lemon thyme that bend with the weight
of their golden bodies, dropping flower to leaf.

Honey seeps slowly from comb to glass
jars like the current of the nearly dry creek.
If it flowed faster, it might clean us all.

The author wishes to extend gratitude to Ross Leckie, Sharon McCartney, and Anne Simpson for their support, and to generous-spirits friends and educators, especially C. Delamere, T. Antoniades, K Raymond, L. Foote, D. Glassco, R. Hales, and J. Whitton.